SO-BWX-776

Ethics and Population Limitation

Daniel Callahan

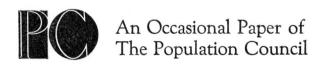

An Occasional Paper of
The Population Council

The Population Council
245 Park Avenue
New York, New York 10017

The Population Council is a foundation established
in 1952 for scientific training and study in population
matters. It endeavors to advance knowledge in the
broad field of population by fostering research, training, and technical consultation and assistance in the
social and biomedical sciences.

John D. Rockefeller 3rd
Chairman of the Board of Trustees
Bernard Berelson, *President*

Distributed for The Population Council by
Key Book Service, Inc., 425 Asylum Street,
Bridgeport, Connecticut 06610.

Standard Book Number: 0-87834-002-5
Library of Congress Catalog Card Number: 78-155736
© Copyright 1971 by The Population Council. All rights
reserved.

Printed in the United States of America by Wm. F. Fell Company,
Philadelphia, Pennsylvania.

CAMROSE LUTHERAN COLLEGE
Library

HQ
764
.C25 /21,620

Contents

GENERAL ETHICAL ISSUES   7
THE DEVELOPMENT OF ETHICAL CRITERIA   10
Deontological Theories   11
    1. Act-deontological Theories
    2. Rule-deontological Theories
Teleological Theories   12
    1. Act-utilitarianism
    2. Rule-utilitarianism

THE ETHICAL ACTORS   16
Individuals (Persons, Couples, Families)   16
    1. The Right of Control
    2. The Right to a Choice of Method
    3. The Right to the Fullest Possible Knowledge
Governments   17
Organizations   20
Recapitulation   22
    1. General Moral Rules
    2. Criteria for Ethical Decision-Making
    3. Rank Order of Preference

SOME SPECIFIC ISSUES   23
Governments   23
Some Formal Criteria and a Ranking of Preference   33
Organizations   36
Freedom and Risk-Taking   40

NOTES   42

Daniel Callahan is Director of the Institute of Society, Ethics and the Life Sciences at Hastings-on-Hudson, New York. This paper was written while Dr. Callahan served as a Staff Associate at The Population Council (1969-70). He is also the author of *Abortion: Law, Choice and Morality* (The Macmillan Company, 1970).

THROUGHOUT its history, the human species has been heavily preoccupied with the conquest of nature and the control of death. Human beings struggled to survive, as individuals, families, tribes, communities and nations. Procreation was an essential part of survival. Food could not be grown, families sustained, individuals supported and industry developed unless there was an unceasing supply of new human beings. The historical result was the assignment of a high value to fertility. It has been thought good to have children: good for the children themselves, for the parents, for the society and for the species. While it may always have been granted that extenuating circumstances could intervene to create temporary contraindications to child-bearing, the value premise endured intact. There remained a presumptive right of individual procreation, a right thought to sustain the high valuation assigned to the outcome: more human beings.

That the premise may now have to be changed, the values shifted, can only seem confounding. As Erik Erikson has urged, it is a risky venture to play with the "fire of creation," especially when the playing has implications for almost every aspect of individual and collective life.[1] The reasons for doing so would have to be grave. Yet the hazards of excessive population growth present such reasons, posing critical dangers to the future of the species, the eco-system, individual liberty and welfare, and the structure of social life. These hazards are serious enough to warrant a re-examination and ultimately a revision of the traditional value assigned to unrestricted procreation and increase in population size.

The main question is the way the revision is to proceed. If the old premise—the unlimited right of and need for

1

procreation—is to be rejected or amended, what alternative premises are available? By what morally legitimate social and political processes, and in the light of what values, are the possible alternatives to be evaluated and action taken? These are ethical questions, bearing on what is taken to constitute the good life, the range and source of human rights and obligations, the requirements of human justice and welfare. If the ethical problems of population limitation could be reduced to one overriding issue, matters would be simplified. They cannot. Procreation is so fundamental a human activity, so wide-ranging in its personal and social impact, that its control poses a wide range of ethical issues. My aim here is primarily to see what some of the different ethical issues are, how an approach to them might be structured, and to propose some solutions.

In a field so ill-defined as "ethics and population limitation," very little by way of common agreement can be taken for granted. One needs to start at the beginning. Some basic assertions can be suggested as "the beginning":

Facts and values. There would be no concern about the ethical issues of population limitation if there did not exist evidence that excessive population growth jeopardizes present and future welfare. Yet the way the evidence is evaluated will be the result of the values and interests brought to bear on the data. Every definition of the "population problem," or of "excessive population growth" will be value-laden, expressive of the ethical orientations of those who do the defining. While everyone might agree that widespread starvation and malnutrition are bad, not everyone will agree that crowding, widespread urbanization, and a loss of primitive forest areas are equally bad. Human beings differ in their assessment of relative goods and evils. To say that "excessive population growth is bad" is to imply that some other state of population growth would be good or better, e.g., an "optimum level of population." But as the demographic discussion of an "optimum" has made clear, so many variables come into play that it may be possible to do no more than specify a direction: "the desirability of a lower rate of growth."[2]

If the way the population problem is defined will reflect value orientations, these same definitions will have direct implications for the way the ethical issues are posed. An apocalyptic reading of the demographic data and projections can, not surprisingly, lead to coercive proposals. Desperate problems are seen to require desperate and otherwise distasteful solutions.[3] Moreover, how the problem is defined, and how the different values perceived to be at stake are weighted, will have direct implications for the priority given to population problems in relationship to other social problems. People might well agree that population is a serious issue, but they might (and often do) say that other issues are comparatively *more* serious.[4] If a low priority is given to population problems, this is likely to affect the perception of the ethical issues at stake.

Why ethical questions arise. Excessive population growth poses ethical questions because it threatens existing or desired human values and goods, and because all or some of the possible solutions to the problem have the potential for posing difficult ethical dilemmas. Choices are required among a variety of values. Excessive population growth poses threats when physical security and health are endangered, political conflicts engendered, economic development hindered, the environment polluted, non-renewable resources rapidly dissipated and psychologically harmful crowding and forced migration intensified—to mention only a few of the possibilities. Any one of these factors, or a combination of them, has the potential to undermine human life. The decision to act or not to act in the face of the threats is an ethical decision. It is a way of affirming where the human good lies and the kinds of obligations individuals and societies have toward themselves and others. A choice in favor of action will, however, mean the weighing of different options, and most of the available options pose ethical dilemmas.

Ethics and politics. The political context of ethical decisions in the population area will often be that of pluralistic societies, where a number of group interests, loyalties and values compete for attention and power. A major difficulty will be that of reconciling different kinds of ethical judgments and value systems. Almost inevitably, then, the ethics of population limitation must encompass the ethics of politics and government as well.

Ends, means and criteria. In making ethical choices, a decision will be needed on (a) the human goods and values which need serving or promoting—the ends; (b) the range of methods and actions consistent and coherent with those ends —the means; and (c) the procedure and rationale to be used in trying to decide both upon ends and means and upon their relationship in specific situations—the ethical criteria for decision-making. A failure to determine the ends, both ultimate and proximate, can make it difficult or impossible to choose the appropriate means. A failure to determine the range of possible means can make it difficult to serve the ends. A failure to specify or articulate the ethical criteria for decision-making can lead to capricious or self-serving choices, as well as placing obstacles in the way of a rational resolution of ethical conflicts.

The last assertion touches directly upon the possibilities of ethical analysis. Among them are these: a heightened sensitivity to the value assumptions latent in our thinking and acting; a greater awareness of the implications for good or evil of the possible lines of conduct open to us; some greater capacity for introducing rigor into our ethical thinking; an expanded talent for devising criteria by which to act. There are also limitations. Ethics has no single methodology; schools and methodologies abound. The history of ethics has been marked by basic disputes about the nature and function of ethics.

There has been, however, general agreement on a few key points. "Traditionally," P. H. Nowell-Smith has remarked, "moral philosophy has always been regarded as a practical science, a 'science' because it was a systematic inquiry the goal of which was knowledge, and 'practical' because the goal was practical knowledge, knowledge of what to do rather than knowledge of what is the case."[5] Yet even though ethics has been directed toward practice and action, its students have agreed that it cannot supply detailed rules about how to act in concrete cases, which can combine a great range of variables; that is why it is often called an art. "A philosopher," to quote Nowell-Smith again, "is not a parish priest or Universal Aunt or Citizens' Advice Bureau."[6]

In the instance of ethics and population limitation, both the possibilities and the limitations of ethics become apparent. In the face of a variety of proposals to solve the population problem, some of them highly coercive, a sensitivity to the ethical issues and some greater rigor in dealing with them is imperative. The most fundamental matters of human life and welfare are at stake. Yet because of the complexity of the problem, including its variability from one nation or geographical region to the next, few hard and fast rules can be laid down about what to do in such and such a place at such and such a time.

Still, since some choices must be made (and not to choose it to make a choice as well), the practical ethical task will be that of deciding upon the available options. While this paper will focus on some of the proposed options to reduce birthrates, they are not the only ones possible. Ralph Potter has discussed some others: "It has generally been assumed that policy must be primarily, if not exclusively, concerned with bringing about a decline in the rate of population increase through a reduction in the birth rate. But there are other choices. It is generally considered desirable but impossible to increase resources at a sufficient pace and through an adequate duration to preserve the present level of living for all within an expanding population. It is generally considered possible but undesirable to omit the requirement that all persons have access to that which is necessary for a good life. There is still the option of redefining what is to be considered necessary for a good life or of foregoing some things necessary for a good life in order to obtain an equitable distribution in a society that preserves the autonomy of parents to determine the size of their families."[7]

A useful way of posing the issue practically is to envision the ethical options ranked on a preferential scale, from the most desirable to the least desirable. For working purposes, I will adopt as my own the formulation of Kenneth E. Boulding: "A moral, or ethical proposition, is a statement about a rank order of preferences among alternatives, which is intended to apply to more than one person."[8] Ethics enters at that point where the preferences are put forward as having a value which transcends individual tastes or inclinations. Implicitly or explicitly, a decision among alternatives becomes an ethical one when it is claimed that one or another alternative *ought* to be chosen, not just by me but by others as well. That is where it differs from tastes or personal likings which, by definition, imply non-obligatory preferences applicable to no more than one person (even if the tastes are shared). The "ought" of ethical propositions can be expressed in the language of "duties," "obligations," or "responsibilities," each of which connotes a level of preferences different from that of personal inclination.

In the face of alternative proposals to reduce population growth, how is a "rank order of preferences" to be determined and obligations sorted out? The answer to this question requires a specification of possible ends, means, and criteria for decision-making; for "preferences," as used here, will refer to all three of these ethical ingredients. It is possible, that is, to make a choice among different ends, different means and different criteria, putting each in some kind of rank order. A first step in the problem of ranking preferences is to delineate some of the major and general ethical issues posed by excessive population growth and the alternative possibilities available to meet it. The second step will be to note some current ethical theories which can be brought to bear in the development of criteria for making decisions and to make a choice among them. The third step will be to sketch the rights of different ethical actors, and their attendant obligations, in population-related ethical decisions. The fourth step will be to list some specific issues of population limitation, attempting to show how the foregoing ethical analysis provides a means of resolution.

GENERAL ETHICAL ISSUES

I will assume at the outset that there is a problem of excessive population growth, serious for the world as a whole (with a 2% annual growth rate), grave for many developing nations (where the growth rate approaches 3% per annum), and possibly harmful for the developed nations as well (with an average 1% growth rate). The threats posed by excessive population growth are numerous: economic, environmental, agricultural, political and socio-psychological. There is considerable agreement that something must be done to meet these threats. For the purpose of ethical analysis, the first question to be asked is: in trying to meet these threats, what human ends are we seeking to serve? Two kinds of human ends can be distinguished: proximate and ultimate.

Among the important proximate ends being sought in attempts to reduce birthrates are (in the developing countries): a raising of literacy rates, a reduction in dependency ratios, the elimination of starvation and malnutrition, more rapid economic development, an improvement in health and welfare services; and (in the developed countries): a maintenance or improvement of the quality of life, the protection of non-renewable resources, the control of environmental pollution. For most purposes, it will be sufficient to cite goals of that sort. But it is critical for ethical purposes to consider not just proximate but ultimate ends as well. For it is legitimate to

ask, of the specified proximate ends, what ultimate human
ends they are meant to serve. Why is it important to raise
literacy rates? Why is it necessary to protect non-renewable
resources? Why ought the elimination of starvation and malnutrition be sought? For the most part, these are questions
which need not be asked or require no elaborate answer. The
ethical importance of such questions is that they force us to
confront the goals of human life. Unless they are confronted
at some point, ethics cannot start or finish.

Philosophically, the problem can be put as one of determining what final values should be pursued. The reason,
presumably, that a reduction in illiteracy rates is sought is
that it is thought valuable for human beings to possess the
means of achieving knowledge. The elimination of starvation
and malnutrition is sought because of a self-evident perception
that human beings must eat to survive. The preservation of
non-renewable resources is necessary in order that human life
can continue through future generations. There is little
argument about the validity of these propositions because
they all presuppose some ultimate human values: knowledge,
life, species survival, for instance. Historically, philosophers
have attempted to specify what, in the name of "the good,"
human beings essentially seek. What do they, in the end,
finally value? The historical list of values is long: life, pleas-
ure, happiness, knowledge, freedom, justice and self-expres-
sion, among others.

This is not the place to enter into a discussion of all these
values and the philosophical history of attempts to specify
and rank them. Suffice it to say that three values have had a
predominant role, at least in the West: freedom, justice and
security/survival. Most pertinently, many of the major ethical
dilemmas posed by the need for population limitation can be
reduced to that of choosing among, ranking and interpreting
these three values. Freedom is a prized value because it is a
condition for self-determination and the achievement of
knowledge. Justice, particularly distributive justice, is prized

because it entails equality of treatment and opportunity and an equitable access to those resources and opportunities necessary for human development. Security/survival is prized because it constitutes a fundamental ground for all human activities.

Excessive population growth poses ethical dilemmas because it forces us to weight and rank these values in trying to find solutions. How much procreative freedom, if any, should be given up in order to insure the security/survival of a nation or a community? How much security/survival can be risked in order to promote distributive justice? How much procreative freedom can be tolerated if it jeopardizes distributive justice?

Ethical dilemmas might be minimized if there was a fixed agreement on the way the three values ought to be ranked. One could say that freedom is so supreme a value that both justice and security/survival should be sacrificed to maintain it. But there are inherent difficulties in taking such a position. It is easily possible to imagine situations where a failure to give due weight to the other values could result in an undermining of the possibility of freedom itself. If people cannot survive at the physical level, it becomes impossible for them to exercise freedom of choice, procreative or otherwise. If the freedom of some is unjustly achieved at the expense of the freedom of others, then the overall benefits of freedom are not maximized. Analogously, if security/survival is given the place of supremacy, situations could arise where this value was used to justify the suppression of freedom or the perpetuation of social injustice. In that case, those suppressed might well ask: why live if one cannot have freedom and justice?

For all these reasons, it is difficult and perhaps unwise to specify a fixed and abstract rank order of preferences among the three values. In some circumstances, each can enter a valid claim against the others. In the end, at the level of abstractions, one is forced to say that all three values are critically important; none can be permanently set aside or minimized. Ethical dilemmas arise because it is often the case that a perfect balance cannot be obtained among them; the price of honoring one is to detract from a full realization of the others.

As I will argue shortly, however, the contemporary rank order of preference in the West, and much of the rest of the world, is to give freedom of choice in family planning the place of primacy. Yet this primacy has been challenged by one group on the grounds that it cannot be relied upon to insure the kind of population control necessary to insure security/survival.[9] And its primacy has been challenged by other groups on the grounds that it diverts attention away from the need for social justice.[10] In the case of both challenges, then, the primacy of freedom is called into question in the name of other values, with different candidates for the place of primacy being put forward.

THE DEVELOPMENT OF ETHICAL CRITERIA

In approaching the task of ranking an order of preference among values in concrete situations, it is necessary to develop ethical criteria. They can then be used in judging the validity of different possible choices. If one asks, of different ethical choices, what is the right thing to do, or what am I obliged to do, no meaningful answer is possible unless there has been a consideration of what might count as a satisfactory answer. What are the ethical criteria for judging among many possible answers?

I propose to analyze that last question in terms of *normative ethics*, particularly that aspect of it which deals with normative theory of obligation. William K. Frankena has provided a representative statement concerning the latter:

> The ultimate concern of the normative theory of obligation is to guide us in the making of decisions and judgments about actions in particular situations. A main concern, of course, is to guide us in

> our capacity as agents trying to decide what we should do in this case and that. But we want to know more than just what we should do in situations before us. We also wish to make judgments about what others should do. . . . We are not just agents in morality; we are also spectators, advisers, instructors, judges and critics. Still, in all of these capacities our primary question is this: how may or should we decide to determine what is morally right for a certain agent (oneself or another, possibly a group or a whole society) to do, or what he morally ought to do, in a certain situation?[11]

Normative theories of obligation are usually divided into two classes, teleological and deontological. Teleological theories hold, in general, that the standard of ethical judgment is the relative balance of good over evil produced: "thus, an act is *right* if and only if it or the rule under which it falls produces, or will probably produce, or is intended to produce *at least as great a balance of good over evil* as any available *alternative;* an act is *wrong* if and only if it does not do so."[12] Deontological theories, by contrast, hold that other factors than the consequences of acts or rules may make them right or obligatory, e.g., their intrinsic validity quite apart from their consequences: "A deontologist contends that it is possible for an action or rule of action to be morally right or obligatory even if it does not promote the greatest possible balance of good over evil for self, society, or universe. It may be right or obligatory simply because of some other fact about it or because of its own nature."[13]

Both deontological and teleological theories have taken different forms (and have been subject to different criticisms).

DEONTOLOGICAL THEORIES

1. Act-deontological theories.

Act-deontologists (E. F. Carritt, H. A. Prichard) maintain that all judgments of obligation ought to be purely particular: in this situation I should do such and such. They affirm that each situation must be judged separately, without recourse to any rules or any attempt to achieve a balance of good over evil. They have been criticized on the grounds that they offer no standards at all for determining right and wrong in particular cases.

2. *Rule-deontological theories.*

Rule-deontologists (Ross, Kant) hold that the standard of ethical obligation consists of rules, either concrete or abstract. They contend that the rules are fundamental, neither inductions from nor to be judged by particular cases. On the contrary, particular cases are to be judged in terms of the rules. The principal objection to these theories lies in the difficulty of framing rules which admit of no exceptions and which will not result in conflict among the rules.

TELEOLOGICAL THEORIES

Teleological theories can, in the first place, be distinguished in terms of the good that one is obliged to promote. *Ethical egoism* (Epicurus, Hobbes, Nietzsche) contends that the pertinent good to be promoted is that of the ethical actor himself —his personal greatest good. *Ethical universalism,* or *utilitarianism* (Bentham, Mill) holds that the ultimate standard is the promotion of the greatest general good. Ethical egoism is open to the objection, among others, that it cannot be to the advantage of an individual that every other individual should single-mindedly pursue his own advantage. *Utilitarianism* (ethical universalism) has had a much larger following in the history of ethics. In Frankena's formulation, "utilitarianism" can be defined as the view "which says the sole ultimate standard of right, wrong, and obligation is the *principle of utility* or *beneficence,* which says quite strictly that the moral end to be sought in all we do is *the greatest possible balance of good over evil* (or the least possible balance of evil over good)."[14] Two views of utilitarianism can be distinguished.

1. *Act-utilitarianism.*

Act-utilitarians hold that, in attempting to determine what is obligatory, one appeals directly to the principle of utility, trying to discover which of the available actions is likely to result in the greatest general balance of good over evil. Pressed to its extreme, this view would not allow us to make use of any rules or to generalize from past experience. It has been criticized on the grounds of its impracticality (for some rules seem necessary).

2. *Rule-utilitarianism.*

In common with rule-deontologists, rule-utilitarians grant a central place to moral rules. They contend that in most if not all situations we are to determine what we ought to do by recourse to a rule (e.g., tell the truth) instead of by determining which particular action will have the best consequences. However, in contrast with rule-deontologism, it stipulates that our rules should be determined by inquiring which rules will promote the greatest general good: "This means that for the rule utilitarian it may be right to obey a rule like telling the truth simply because it is so useful to have the rule, even when, in the particular case in question, telling the truth does not lead to the best consequences."[15]

There are at least two major difficulties with rule-utilitarianism. One has to do with the interpretation of the principle of utility. What is to count as the "general good"? The other concerns the problem of justice. A rule may, for instance, maximize the general amount of good in the world and yet result in a mal-distribution of the good; that is, it might be unjust in its effects, benefiting most but not all. The problem is that the principle of utility tells us to maximize the good but provides no directions in choosing how to distribute the good; an independent principle of justice is needed for that purpose. Accordingly, a *mixed deontological theory* has been proposed: "there are at least two basic and independent principles of morality, that of beneficence or utility which tells us to maximize the total amount of good in the world . . . and that of justice. . . . This theory instructs us to determine what is right or wrong in particular situations, normally at least, by consulting rules such as we usually associate with morality; but it goes on to say that the way to tell what rules we should live by is to see which rules best fulfill the joint requirements of utility and justice."[16] A similar theory has been proposed by Henry D. Aiken, only his version adds liberty as independent principle. The principle of utility then comes to function not as a test of the independent principles —for neither justice nor liberty can or ought to be justified on utilitarian grounds—but, instead, "is at best to be viewed as a principle for the making of exceptions to other principles that are themselves independently binding."[17]

For the purposes of this paper, I will work with the last-mentioned position, a *mixed deontological theory,* adapting it somewhat to my own purposes. As "independent principles" I will count the three mentioned earlier: freedom (liberty), justice, security/survival. Each, I believe, is best justified in its own terms, not in terms of its utility; that is, each has a value independent of its utility. Yet since ethical dilemmas arise because of real or apparent conflicts between and among these principles, the principle of utility can be used in those situations where exceptions to one or another principles appear in order. Thus when conflicts arise, it is legitimate to turn to the utilitarian principle as a standard for testing proposed resolutions. In a situation posing a conflict between the principle of procreative freedom and the principle of security/survival, for instance, one can turn to the principle of utility to see whether the demands of security/survival would warrant taking exception to the otherwise valid principle of freedom. Would a limitation of freedom serve to increase the balance of good over evil, in accordance with the principle of utility?

The above-specified mixed deontological theory will, then, serve as my general ethical criteria for deciding among specific population limitation proposals. *Put formally, it can be understood to mean that one is obliged to act in such a way that the fundamental values of freedom, justice and security/*

CAMROSE LUTHERAN COLLEGE
Library

survival are to be respected and, in case of conflict, that one or more of these values can be limited if and only if it can be shown that such a course will serve to increase the balance of good over evil. Put in the terminology employed by Boulding: rank order of preference among alternatives should go to those which, consistent with the intrinsic values of freedom, justice and security/survival, increase the balance of good over evil. In situations of conflict among the principles, those alternatives are to be preferred which minimize the limitations on the three values.

A further specification is necessary. I argued earlier that it is difficult and perhaps unwise to attempt a fixed and abstract ranking of the values of freedom, justice, and security/survival. However, in the area of family planning and population limitation a number of national and international declarations have served to give a primacy of place to individual freedom. The Declaration of the 1968 United Nations International Conference on Human Rights is representative: ". . . couples have a basic human right to decide freely and responsibly on the number and spacing of their children and a right to adequate education and information in this respect."[18] While this primacy has been challenged,[19] it retains its position, serving as the ethical foundation of both domestic and foreign family planning and population policies. Accordingly, it will be argued here (a) that the burden of proof on proposals to limit freedom of choice (whether on the grounds of justice or security/survival) rests with those who make the proposals, but that (b) this burden can, under specified conditions, be discharged if it can be shown that a limitation of freedom of choice in the name of justice or security/survival would tend to increase the general balance of good over evil. This is only to say that while the present international "rank order of preference" gives individual freedom the primary place, it is possible to imagine circumstances which would require a revision of the ranking.

THE ETHICAL ACTORS

One way of approaching the normative issues of ranking preferences in population limitation programs and proposals is by locating the key ethical actors, those who can be said to have obligations. Three groups of actors can be identified: individuals (persons, couples, families), the officers and agents of voluntary (private-external) organizations, and responsible government officials. What are the ethical obligations of each of the actors? What is the right or correct course of conduct for them? I will approach these questions by first trying to define some general rights and obligations for each set of actors and then, in the final section of the paper, by offering some suggested resolutions of a number of specific issues.

INDIVIDUALS (PERSONS, COUPLES, FAMILIES)

We begin with individuals because it has already been contended that, in the ranking of values, individual freedom of choice has been accorded an international primacy; and it is individuals who procreate. What are the rights and obligations of individuals with regard to procreation?

Individuals have the right voluntarily to *control* their own fertility in accordance with their personal preferences and convictions (whatever their source).[20] This right logically extends to a *choice of methods* to achieve the desired control and the right to the *fullest possible knowledge* of available methods and their consequences (medical, social, economic and demographic, among others):

The right of control: this right implies non-interference and non-coercion on the part of others (individuals, organizations and governments); it also entails the obligation of others to respect, protect and advance this right.

The right to a choice of methods: this right implies the availability of a range of methods; it entails the obligation of others (particularly governments) to take those steps necessary to provide the required range of methods.

The right to the fullest possible knowledge: this right implies an access to knowledge, in order that the choices made will reflect an awareness of options and of the consequences of the options; it entails an obligation on the part of others to share the knowledge they possess fully and truthfully, not only when such knowledge is requested but also on their own initiative when not requested.

Individuals have the obligation to care for the needs of and respect the rights of their existing children (intellectual, emotional and physical); and, in their decision to have a child (or another child), to determine if they will be able to care for the needs and respect the rights of the child-to-be. Since individuals are obliged to respect the rights of others, they are obliged in their conduct to act in such a way that these rights are not jeopardized. In determining family size, this means they are obliged to exercise their own freedom of choice in such a way that they do not curtail the freedom of others. They are obliged, in short, to respect the requirements of the common good in their exercise of free choice.[21] The source of these obligations is the rights of others.

GOVERNMENTS

The role of governments in promoting the welfare of its citizens has long been recognized. It is only fairly recently, however, that governments have come to take a leading role in an anti-natalist control of fertility. This has come about by the establishment in a number of countries of national family planning programs and the establishment of national population policies. While many countries still do not have such policies, few international objections have been raised against the right of nations to develop them. So far, most government population policies have rested upon and been justified in terms of an extension of freedom of choice. Increasingly, though, it is being recognized that since demographic trends can have a significant impact on national welfare, it is within the right of nations to adopt policies designed to reduce birth rates and slow population growth.

A preliminary question must, therefore, be asked. Is there any special reason to presume or suspect that governmental intervention in the area of individual procreation and national fertility patterns raises problems which, *in kind,* are significantly different from other kinds of interventions? To put the question another way, can the ethico-political problems which arise in this area be handled by historically and traditionally available principles of political ethics, or must an entirely new form of ethics be devised?

I can see no special reason to think that the formation of interventionist anti-natalist national population policies poses any unique *theoretical* difficulties. To be sure, the problem of a perceived need to reduce population growth is historically new; there exists no developed political or ethico-political tradition dealing with the specific problem. Yet the principle of governmental intervention into procreation-related behavior has a long historical precedent: in earlier pro-natalist population policies, in the legal regulation of marriage, and in laws designed to regulate sexual behavior. It seems a safe generalization to say that governments have felt (and generally been given) as much right to intervene in this area as in any other where individual and collective welfare appears at stake. That new forms of intervention may seem called for or be proposed (i.e., in an anti- rather than pro-natalist direction) does not mean that a new ethical or political principle is at issue. No such principle at least appears immediately evident.

Yet if it is possible to agree that no new problems of principles are raised, it is still possible to argue that a further extension of an old principle—the right of government intervention into procreation-related behavior—would be wrong. Indeed, it is an historical irony that after a long international struggle to establish the freedom of choice of individuals to control their own fertility, that freedom should immediately be challenged in the name of the population crisis. Irony or not, there is no cause to be surprised by such a course of events. The history of human liberty is studded with instances in which, for a variety of reasons, it has been possible to say that liberty is a vital human good and yet that, for the sake of other goods, restriction of liberty seems required. A classical argument for the need of a government is that a formal and public apparatus is necessary to regulate the use of individual liberty for the sake of the common good.

It will, in any case, be the premise of the ensuing discussion that governments have as much right to intervene in pro-creation-related behavior as they do in other areas of behavior affecting the general welfare. This right extends to the control of fertility generally and the control of individual fertility in particular. The critical issue is the way in which this right is to be exercised—its conditions and limits—and that can only be approached by first noting some general issues bearing on the restriction of individual freedom of choice by governments.

Governments have the right to take those steps necessary to insure the preservation and promotion of the common good: the protection and advancement of the right to life, liberty and property. The maintenance of an orderly and just political and legal system, of internal and external security, and an equitable distribution of goods and resources are encompassed within its rights. Its obligations are to act in the interests of the people, to observe human rights, to respect national values and traditions and to guarantee justice and equality. Since excessive population growth can touch upon all these elements of national life, responses to population problems will encompass both the rights and obligations of governments. As will be argued in more detail below, however, governmental acts should represent collective national decisions and be subject to a number of controlling stipulations.

ORGANIZATIONS

Democratic societies are marked by the existence of private, voluntary organizations. Their right to existence is legally guaranteed. They are free to act as they see fit provided they act within the law. Morally, they are required to act in accordance with principles of human rights and dignity. Along with other voluntary associations, organizations working in the field of population have the same general rights as other associations: the right to freedom of speech and action, freedom from unjust and illegal governmental interference, the right to press their own viewpoint. Specifically, voluntary population organizations have the right to engage in research, to provide information, assistance and support when requested, the right to persuade individuals, other organizations and governments to accept offers of information and assistance.

The obligations of private organizations are more complex. They fall into three categories: obligations toward individuals, laws and governments.

Private organizations working in the population field have the same obligations as individuals: to respect the freedom of choice of other individuals. Respect for this freedom requires more than a merely perfunctory or formalistic attempt to determine the wishes or values of another. While it is the right of organizations to engage in rational persuasion of others, they should bear in mind that, even in situations where there is in principle the right of individual decision-making, there can often be an inequality of power relationships. Uneducated people often feel at a disadvantage in their relationship with educated elites. They may feel intimidated even if that is not the intention of the elite person with whom they interact. The extensive literature on the problem of "voluntary consent" has detailed both the difficulties in adequately defining the concept and in assuring that such consent has genuinely been obtained. It is not enough simply to ask for consent and to get an answer. More than that, it is necessary for those seeking consent to make a serious effort to determine, so far as possible, if verbal responses adequately reflect a full freedom of choice. Complaints of minority and other groups that they are sometimes at a disadvantage in the face of the persuasive efforts of majorities and elites must be taken seriously.

An important component of freedom of choice is the right of the individual to have *his* perception of situations count; that perception should be the starting point. When assistance is being offered to individuals, organizations also have the obligation to make known to them the possible or likely consequences of their choices. They have the right to point out the advantages as they see them; they have the obligation to point out possible disadvantages.

The obligations of voluntary organizations toward existing laws, whether in their own or in other countries, are complicated by the fact that not all laws are just, representative of public opinion or rational. If it is taken to be the human right of individuals to control their own fertility, it would seem morally permissible for an organization to press for the fulfillment of those rights even if in opposition to existing laws. But this course would be permissible only if it was determined that the people of an area or nation were seeking those rights, and that all efforts to have the laws changed had failed. Politically of course any attempt to circumvent laws could be exceedingly unwise; and it would be necessary to determine if a circumvention of laws for the sake of one set of human rights would be worth the threat that the principle of circumvention would introduce into a social order. It could only be justified as a last resort and only if some central human values seemed to be at stake.

Normally, organizations would be obliged to respect not only existing laws but also community attitudes and mores. This would particularly be the case where the organizations are external to the communities or nations within which they operate. They cannot presume an automatic right to intervene in either the internal or external affairs of a society. On the contrary, societies have the right to self-determination, including the right to exclude those outside of the society they choose not to admit.

The obligations of voluntary organizations toward governments whom they assist pose still further complications. Organizations have the right to provide information so long as they do not infringe the rights of individuals and the rights of governments to implement a nations desire for self-determination. If a government has not expressly forbidden an organization to assist in the development of programs and policies, they ought feel no compunction about doing so. The determining element would be the desires of the people.

RECAPITULATION

It is time to pause and recapitulate the points so far made. This will be done by offering some summary propositions, which I will then use to suggest solutions to some specific ethical issues.

1. General moral rules

(a.) *Individuals* have the right to freedom of procreative choice; they have the obligation to respect the freedom of others and the requirements of the common good.

(b.) *Governments* have the right to take those steps necessary to secure a maximization of freedom, justice and security/survival; they have the obligation to act in such a way that freedom and justice are protected and security/survival enhanced.

(c.) *Organizations* have the right to act as they see fit providing that they respect the rights of individual and governments; they have the obligation to respect those rights.

2. Criteria for ethical decision-making

(a.) One (individual, government, organization) is obliged to act in such a way that the fundamental values of freedom, justice, and security/survival are respected.

(b.) In cases of conflict, one is obliged to act in such a way that any limitation of one or more of the three fundamental values—a making of exceptions to the rules concerning these values—continues to respect the values and can be justified because it promises to increase the balance of good over evil.

3. Rank order of preference

(a.) Those choices of action ought to be preferred which give a primacy of place to the value of freedom of choice.

(b.) If conditions appear to require a limitation of freedom, this should be done in such a way as to minimize the direct and indirect harmful consequences, and be just in the chosen means of limitation; the less the harm, the higher the ranking.

SOME SPECIFIC ISSUES

Since it has already been contended that individual freedom of choice has a primacy, the ethical issues to be specified here will concentrate on those posed for governments and organizations. And this focus will, in any event, serve to test the limits of individual freedom.

GOVERNMENTS

Faced with an excessive population growth, a variety of courses are open to governments. They can do nothing at all. They can institute, develop or expand voluntary family planning programs. They can attempt to implement proposals which go "beyond family planning."[22]

Would it be ethically right for a nation experiencing excessive population growth to do nothing at all? Let us assume that a government had sound evidence that present and projected growth pose a direct and relatively immediate threat to physical life. In that event, and since it is the obligation of government to do what is necessary to protect security/survival, it would be wrong for a government to do nothing. Moreover, when it can be shown that the people desire the knowledge and means of reducing the size of their families, a government would be derelict in its duty to the right of individuals to procreative freedom if it did nothing. Is it possible to imagine circumstances under which a government would be justified in doing nothing? Perhaps so, if, for instance, a government could show that its decision to do nothing truly represented the desires of those it governed. However, since a decision to do nothing would have profound implications for future generations, it is difficult to see how it could justify decisions which would, in effect, preempt their right to freedom and security/survival.

Is it right for a government, in response to excessive population growth, to institute, develop and implement a voluntary family planning program? Yes, for this is one way for a government to respect and make effective the individual's right to free choice. Indeed, quite apart from a population problem, governments have an obligation to respect freedom of choice in family planning. If knowledge does not exist of the possible choices, or the means do not exist to implement the choices, then the freedom is nullified; hence, governments appear to have an obligation to make the freedom efficacious, by the establishment of a program. If it could be shown that voluntary organizations are meeting the need, this would diminish the government's obligation to act.

Is it right to include sterilization and abortion in voluntary government family planning programs? Sterilization appears to pose no special ethical issues insofar as its choice remains wholly voluntary and that choice is made upon the best available knowledge of the consequences for the individual. Family planning programs would, of course, have the obligation of taking the initiative if necessary in pointing out the consequences; otherwise, the individual's capacity to make a prudent choice would be limited. To be sure, it is the obligation of those responsible for family planning programs to make available to individuals their knowledge of the consequences (medical, psychological, etc.) of any method included in their program. Abortion poses more difficult problems, primarily because many individuals and some religions consider abortion the taking of human life. However, if abortion is legal in a country and if its use remains voluntary in a family planning program, it would seem ethically right to include it in a program.[23]

Would it be right for governments to go "beyond family planning" if the gravity of excessive population growth could be shown? This question conceals a great range of issues. Who would decide if governments have this right? Of all the possible ways of going "beyond family planning," which could be most easily justified and which would be the hardest to justify? How much of a showing of the gravity of the problem would be necessary? As a general proposition, it is possible ethically to say that governments would have the right to go beyond family planning. The obligation of governments to protect fundamental values could require that they set aside the primacy of freedom in order to protect justice and security/survival. But everything would depend upon the way in which they proposed to do so. Let us examine some of the possibilities, attempting at the end to specify an ethical "rank order of preference":

Would it be right for governments to establish involuntary fertility controls? These might include (if technically feasible) the use of a mass "fertility control agent," the licensing of the right to have children, compulsory temporary or permanent sterilization, or compulsory abortion.[24] Proposals of this kind have been put forth primarily as "last resort" methods, often in the context that human survival may be at stake. "Compulsory control of family size is an unpalatable idea to many," the Ehrlichs have written, "but the alternatives may be much more horrifying . . . human survival seems certain to require population control programs. . . . ."[25] Their own suggestion is manifestly coercive: "If . . . relatively uncoercive laws should fail to bring the birth rate under control, laws could be written that would make the bearing of a third child illegal and that would require an abortion to terminate all such pregnancies."[26]

That last suggestion requires examination. Let us assume for the moment that the scientific case has been made that survival itself is at stake, and that the administrative and enforcement problems admit of a solution. Even so, some basic ethical issues would remain. "No one," the United Nations has declared, "shall be subjected to torture or to cruel, inhuman or degrading treatment or punishment."[27] It is hard to see how compulsory abortion, requiring governmental invasion of a woman's body, could fail to qualify as "inhuman or degrading . . . punishment." Moreover, it is difficult to see how this kind of suggestion can be said to respect in any way the values of freedom and justice. It removes free choice altogether, and in its provision for an abortion of the third child makes no room for distributive justice at all; its burden would probably fall upon the poorest and least educated. It gives security/survival the primacy but to such an extent and in such a way that the other values are ignored altogether. But could not one say, where survival itself is at stake, that this method would increase the balance of good over evil? The case would not be easy to make, (a) because survival is not the *only* human value at stake, (b) because the social consequences of such a law could be highly destructive (e.g., the inevitably massive fear and anxiety about third pregnancies which would result from such a law), and (c) because it would be almost impossible to show that this is the *only* method which would or could work to achieve the desired reduction in birth rates.

Would it be right for governments to develop "positive" incentive programs, designed to provide people with money or goods in return for a regulation of their fertility behavior? These might include payments for sterilization, for the use of contraceptives, for periods of non-pregnancy or non-birth, for family planning bonds or "responsibility prizes."[28] In principle, incentive schemes are non-coercive, i.e., people are not forced to take advantage of the incentive. Instead, the point of an incentive is to give them a choice they did not previously have.

Yet there are a number of ethical questions about incentive plans. To whom would they most appeal? Presumably, their greatest appeal would be to the poor, those who want or need the money or goods offered by an incentive program; they would hold little appeal for the affluent, who already have these things. Yet if the poor desperately need the money or goods offered by the incentive plan, it is questionable whether, in any real sense, they have a free choice. Their material needs may make the incentive seem coercive to them. Thus, if it is only or mainly the poor who would find the inducements of an incentive plan attractive, a question of distributive justice is raised. Because of their needs, the poor have less choice than the rich about accepting or rejecting the incentive; this could be seen as a form of exploitation of poverty. In sum, one can ask whether incentive schemes are or could be covertly coercive, and whether they are or could be unjust?[29] If so, then while they may serve the need for security/survival, they may do so at the expense of freedom and justice.

At least three responses seem possible. First, if the need for security/survival is desperate, incentive schemes might well appear the lesser evil in comparison with more overtly coercive alternatives. Second, the possible objections to incentive schemes could be reduced if, in addition to having the benefit of reducing births, they met additional needs as well. For instance, a "family planning bond" program would have the additional benefit of providing old-age security.[30] And any one of the programs might be defended on the grounds that those who take advantage of it actually want to control births in any case (if this can be shown). Third, much could depend upon the size of the incentive benefits. At present, most incentive programs offer comparatively small rewards; one may doubt that they offer great dilemmas for individuals or put them in psychologically difficult straits. The objection of coercion would become most pertinent if it can be shown that the recipients of an incentive believe they have no real choice in the matter (because of their desperate poverty or the size of the incentive); so far, this does not appear to be the case.[31]

While ethical objections have been leveled at incentive programs because of some experienced corrupt practices in their implementation, this seems to raise less serious theoretical issues. Every program run by governments is subject to corruption; but there are usually ways of minimizing them (by laws and review procedures, for instance). Corruption, I would suggest, becomes a serious theoretical issue only when and if it can be shown that a government program is *inherently* likely to create a serious, inescapable and socially damaging system of corruption. This does not appear to be the case with those incentive programs so far employed or proposed.

Would it be right for governments to institute "negative" incentive programs? These could take the form of a withdrawal of child or family allowances after x number of children, a withdrawal of maternity benefits after x number, or a reversal of tax benefits, favoring those with small families.[32] A number of objections have been leveled at such proposed programs. They are directly coercive, in that they deprive people of a free choice about how many children they will have by imposing a penalty on excess procreation; thus they do not give a primacy to freedom of choice. They can also violate the demands of justice, especially in those cases where the burden of the penalties would fall upon those children who would lose benefits available to their siblings. And the penalties would probably be more onerous to the poor than to the rich, further increasing the injustice. Finally, from quite a different perspective, the social consequences of such programs could be most undesirable. They could, for instance, have the effect of worsening the health and welfare of those mothers, families and children who would lose needed social and welfare benefits. Moreover, such programs could be patently unjust in those places where effective contraceptives do not exist (most places at present). For in that case, people would be penalized for having children which the available birth control methods do not effectively allow them to avoid.

It is possible to imagine ways of reducing the force of these objections. If the penalties were quite mild, more symbolic than actual (as Garret Hardin has proposed), the objection from the viewpoint of free choice would be less; and the same would apply to the objection from the viewpoint of justice.[33] Moreover, if the penalty system was devised in such a way that the welfare of children and families would not be harmed, the dangerous social consequences would be mitigated. Much would depend, in short, upon the actual provisions of the penalty plan and the extent to which it could minimize injustice and harmful social consequences. Nonetheless, penalty schemes raise some serious ethical problems. They would seem justifiable only if it could be shown that survival/security was at stake and that, in their application, they could give due respect to freedom and justice. Finally, it would have to be shown that, despite their disadvantages, they promised to increase the balance of good over evil—which would include a calculation of the harm done to freedom and justice and a weighing of other possibly harmful social consequences.

Would it be right for governments to introduce anti-natalist shifts in social and economic institutions? Among such shifts might be a raising of marriage ages, manipulation of the family structure in a nonfamilial direction, and bonuses for delayed marriage.[34] The premise of these proposals is that fertility patterns are influenced by the context in which choices are made, and that some contexts (e.g., higher female employment) are anti- rather than pro-natalist. Thus, instead of intervening directly into the choices women make, they would alter the environment of choice; freedom of individual choice would remain. The attractiveness of these proposals lies in their non-interference with choice; they do not envision coercion. But they are not without their ethical problems, at least in some circumstances. A too-heavy weighting of the environment of choice in an anti-natalist direction would be tantamount to an interference with freedom of choice—even if, technically, a woman could make a free choice. In some situations, a manipulation of the institution of marriage (e.g., raising the marriage age) could be unjust, especially when there exist no available social options for women other than marriage.

The most serious problems, however, lie in the potential social consequences of changes in basic social institutions. What would be the long-term consequences of a radical manipulation of family structure for the male-female relationship, for the welfare of children, for the family? One might say that the consequences would be good or bad, but the important point is that they would have to be weighed. Should some of them appear bad, one would then have to justify these consequences as entailing a lesser evil than a continuation of high fertility rates. If some of the changes promised to be all-but-irreversible once introduced, the justification would have to be all the greater. However, if the introduction of shifts in social institutions had some advantages in addition to anti-natalism—for instance, greater freedom for women, a value in its own right—these could be taken to offset some other possibly harmful consequences.

Would it be right for the government of a developed nation to make the establishment of a population control program in a developing nation a condition of extending food aid?[35] This would be extremely difficult to justify on ethical grounds. At the very least, it would constitute an interference in a nation's right to self-determination.[36] Even more seriously, it would be a direct exploitation of one nation's poverty in the interests of another nation's concept of what is good for it; and that would be unjust. Finally, I would argue that,

on the basis of Article 3 of the Universal Declaration of
Human Rights, a failure to provide needed food aid would
be a fundamental violation of the right to life (when that aid
could, without great cost to the benefactor nation, be given).[37]
The argument that such aid, without an attendant population
control program, would only make the problem worse in the
long run, is defective. Those already alive, and in need of
food, have a right to security/survival. To willfully allow
them to die, or to deprive them of the necessities of life, in
the name of saving even more lives at a later date cannot be
justified in the name of a greater balance of good over evil.
There could be no guarantee that those lives would be saved,
and there would be such a violation of the rights of the living
(including the right to life) that fundamental human values
would be sacrificed.

*Would it be right for a government to institute a population
control program which goes "beyond family planning" for the
sake of racist or self-interested political ends?* No, because
racism is itself ethically illegitimate, involving gross injustice
and deprivation of freedom. The use of population programs
for self-interested political ends (e.g., the maintenance of a
government regime, the protection of the interests of an elite
group) is no less wrong, a violation also of freedom and justice.

But what of those situations where only a voluntary family
planning program is envisaged, a program which has the
virtue of providing assistance known to be desired but which
also, as a vice, happens to serve the racist or political interests
of those establishing the program? A problem of this kind
indicates the shortcomings of using a criterion so general as
the "balance of good over evil." My own conclusion is that
it would be wrong for a government to introduce such a
program unless it made known its ulterior political purposes
in doing so. Otherwise, those taking part in the program
would not have a full knowledge of the possible consequences
of their choices; and that would be to deprive them of an
important element of freedom of choice—knowledge of con-

sequences. Put another way, a "voluntary" program which concealed the motives behind the program and its political implications, would not be genuinely voluntary.

Would it be right for a government to institute programs which go "beyond family planning"—particularly in a coercive direction—for the sake of future more than of present generations? This is a particularly difficult question, in great part because the status of the rights of yet-to-be-born generations has never been philosophically, legally or ethically analyzed in any great depth.[38] On the one hand, it is evident that the actions of one generation can have profound effects on the options available to future generations. And just as those living owe much of their own welfare to those who preceded them historically (beginning with their parents), so too, the living would seem to have obligations to those yet unborn. On the other hand, though, the living do themselves have rights, not just potential but actual. To set aside these rights, necessary for the dignity of the living, in favor of those not yet living would, I think, be to act arbitrarily.

A general solution might, however, be suggested. While the rights of the living should take clear precedence over the rights of unborn generations, the living have an obligation to refrain from actions which would endanger the possibility of future generations enjoying the same rights they presently enjoy. This means, for instance, that the present generation should not exhaust non-renewable resources, irrevocably pollute the environment or procreate to such an extent that future generations will be left with an unmanageably large number of people. All of these obligations imply a possible restriction of freedom. However, since the present generation does have the right to make use of natural resources and to procreate, it must be demonstrated (and not just asserted) that the conduct of the present generation is such as to pose a direct threat to the possibility of future generations enjoying similar rights. In a word, the present generation cannot be deprived of rights on the basis of vague speculations about the future or uncertain projections into the future (see "freedom and risk-taking," p. 40).

Do governments have the right unilaterally to introduce programs which go "beyond family planning"? It is doubtful that they do. Article 21 of the Universal Declaration of Human Rights asserts that "Everyone has the right to take part in the government of his country, directly or through freely chosen representatives. . . . The will of the people shall be the basis of the authority of government."[39] No reason is evident why matters pertaining to fertility control should be exempt from the requirements of this right. By direct implication, not only measures which go beyond family planning, but family planning programs as well require the sanction of the will of the people and the participation of the people in important decisions.

SOME FORMAL CRITERIA AND A RANKING OF PREFERENCES

The preceding list of specific issues by no means exhausts the full range of possible ethical issues pertaining to governmental action; it is meant to be illustrative only of some of the major issues. Moreover, the suggested solutions are no less illustrative. The complexities of specific situations could well lead to a modification of any one of them. That is why ethical analysis can *never* say exactly what ought to be done in *x* place, at *y* time, by *z* people. It can suggest general guidelines only.

I want now to propose some general ethical guidelines for governmental action, putting them in the form of a "rank order of preferences," from the most preferable to the least preferable.

1. Given the primacy accorded to freedom of choice, governments have an obligation to do everything within their power to protect, enhance and implement freedom of choice in family planning. This means the establishment, as the first order of business, of effective voluntary family planning programs.

2. If it turns out that voluntary programs are not effective in reducing excessive population growth, then governments have the right, as the next step, to introduce programs which go "beyond family planning." However, in order to justify the introduction of such programs, it must be shown that voluntary methods have been adequately and fairly tried, and yet nonetheless have failed and promise to continue to fail. It is highly doubtful that, at present, such programs have "failed"; they have not been tried in any massive and systematic way.[40]

3. In choosing among possible programs which go "beyond family planning," governments have an obligation to first try those which, comparatively, most respect freedom of choice (i.e., are the least coercive). For instance, they should try "positive" incentive programs and manipulation of social structures before resorting to "negative" incentive programs and involuntary fertility controls.

4. Further, if circumstances force a government to choose programs which are either quasi- or wholly coercive, they can justify such programs if and only if a number of prior conditions have been met:

(a) If, in the light of the primacy of free choice, government has discharged the burden of proof necessary to justify a limitation of free choice; and the burden of proof is on the government. This burden may be discharged by a demonstration that continued unrestricted liberty poses a direct threat to distributive justice or security/survival. Restrictions on liberty can only be instituted when *essential* requirements of the common good are threatened.

(b) If, in light of the right of citizens to take part in the government of their country:

—the proposed limitations on freedom promise to increase the sum total, in the long run, of options of choice. Thus even if set aside temporarily, a commitment to freedom of choice must remain influential.

—decisions to limit freedom are collective decisions.

—the limitations on freedom are in accord with the principle of due process of law and distributive justice. The limitations must be legally regulated and the burden must fall upon all equally.

—the chosen means of limitation respect human dignity, which will be here defined as respecting those rights specified in the United Nations "Declaration of Human Rights." The end—even security/survival—does not justify the means when the means violate human dignity and when the means logically contradicts the end.

As a general rule, the more coercive the proposed plan, the more stringent the conditions necessary to justify and regulate the coercion should be. In addition, as one moves through a continuum of possible programs, from the least coercive to the most coercive, there is an obligation to take account of the possible social consequences of different programs, consequences over and above their impact on freedom, justice and security/survival. Thus if it appears that some degree of coercion is required, that policy or program should be chosen which:

- entails the least amount of coercion.

- limits the coercion to the fewest possible cases.

- is most problem-specific.

- allows the most room for dissent of conscience.

- limits the coercion to the narrowest possible range of human rights.

- least threatens human dignity.

- least establishes precedents for other forms of coercion.

- is most quickly reversible if conditions change.

While it is true to say that social, cultural and political life requires, and has always required, some degree of limitation on individual liberty—and thus some coercion—that precedent does not by itself automatically justify the introduction of new limitations.[41] Every proposal for a new limitation must be justified in its own terms—the specific form of the proposed limitation must be specifically justified. It must be proved that it represents the least possible coercion, that it minimizes injustice to the greatest extent possible, that it gives the greatest promise of enhancing security/survival, and that its harmful consequences (short- and long-term) are the fewest possible.

ORGANIZATIONS

The ethical problems facing private, voluntary non-governmental organizations working in the population and family planning field are somewhat different from those facing governments, though most of the same criteria will apply.

Do organizations have the obligation to provide information on the consequences (medical, social, etc.) of the programs and methods they support and promote? Yes, since a knowledge of these consequences will or should be an important part of a decision to accept the assistance offered by an organization. Without knowledge, the freedom of recipients is curtailed by real or comparative ignorance. The obligation to support the freedom of others cannot be discharged if available knowledge is withheld. But what if the consequences of different kinds of assistance and methods are not known? In that case, the obligation would be discharged by pointing out that fact. Is there an obligation to provide a knowledge of consequences even if a recipient of aid does not ask for it? Yes, if the known data is of a kind which might significantly influence a decision whether to accept the aid or not.

Is it right for organizations to assist dictatorial governments in the development of population control programs? Everything would depend upon the conditions under which assistance was provided. By definition, dictatorial governments deprive people of the right to take part in the government of their country. Direct assistance to such governments can readily (and often justly) be considered a means of aiding and abetting them in their maintenance of power.

Yet a distinction can be made between helping a government and helping the people themselves. If, in the instance of population control, the goals of a dictatorial government reflect the desires of the people, assistance could be ethically legitimate. The critical question would be whether the people want the kind of assistance and the program the government proposes to help provide them. It is their freedom, not that of the government, which is important. In case of doubt, the granting of a request ought to be conditional upon the right of the organization to conduct a survey to determine what the people want. In cases where there is reason to think that the government has ulterior motives in wanting to see population control programs introduced, it would become imperative to inform potential recipients of aid of the possible political consequences of their acceptance. Only in that way could their full freedom be protected.

Is it right for organizations to advocate that methods or programs be adopted abroad which are not acceptable at home? Some distinctions need to be made here. For instance, abortion is not yet legally acceptable in all areas in the United States; yet the right exists to advocate the legalization of abortion. There is no reason why it could not be advocated for other countries—as long as those countries remain fully free to reject it. Thus a general principle: it is right to advocate for other countries anything which can legally be advocated for this country.

Yet other kinds of cases present themselves. In the United States it is considered medically vital that women who make use of oral contraceptives be carefully supervised and given regular medical examinations. Would it be right to promote the use of such contraceptives in countries which could not manage medical supervision or examinations? Only under one condition: that those who would use the contraceptives be informed that there is some medical risk and that, normally, their use should medically be monitored—something which cannot be done in their case should they choose to use the contraceptive. Any other course would be a violation of the recipient's right to freedom, which includes knowledge of possible consequences.

What about the testing of contraceptives in countries which have less stringent drug-testing laws than does the United States?[42] There is no international legal requirement that all nations have the same drug-testing standards as the United States. At the same time, though, the point of the American standards is to protect experimental subjects from harm and abuse. It would ethically be wrong to support experiments which did not protect subjects or have their voluntary consent, regardless of local laws on the subject. Nor can it be plausibly argued that the dangers of excessive population growth warrant a lessening of the moral standards which should accompany any drug testing. A whole range of diseases and pathologies threaten human life, any one of which might be used to claim that a warrant exists for lower standards; it would seem wise that, if exceptions are not made in those cases, they should not be made in this one.

Is it right for organizations to use funds contributed by donors with ulterior motives? Yes, if a number of conditions are met: if the motives do not violate freedom and justice; if those who are to be the primary beneficiaries of the funds are informed of the motives of those who provided them; if the recipient organization informs the donor that the funds will be used to further the ends of the organization rather than the goals of the donor; if the use to be made of the funds does nothing to violate the U.N. "Declaration of Human Rights."

Do organizations working in the population field have any obligation for related social and political reforms? Within limits, there are some obligations. When social and political reforms have as their aim the realization of basic human rights, e.g., life, liberty and security, any organization whose activities could have an influence on their achievement has an obligation to do nothing which would hinder a realization of that goal. Moreover, within the limits of their capability, they have an obligation to make every effort to see that their own efforts make a contribution to the needed social and political reforms. At the very least, they have an obligation to act in ways consistent with their own stated ultimate goals. For instance, if one of the ultimate goals of a population organization is the reduction of poverty or an improvement of the quality of life, then they would seem obliged to take whatever steps they could to make certain that their own efforts did not hinder the achievement of that goal. If it could be shown, for example, that a population control program would, in an oligarchical society, serve mainly to increase the wealth of the rich, then an organization would be justified in seeking assurances that the assistance it renders would be made part of a program of social reform, justly distributing any improvement in the GNP which might stem from its efforts.[43] In situations where social reform is badly needed, one concrete way of testing whether the activities of a population organization are a hindrance to social and political reforms would be by consulting those within a nation most active in pressing for those reforms. What do they have to say about the activities of the organization?

Do population organizations have the right to advocate and promote population control if they know that such control could, in some societies, lead to vast long-run cultural changes? As long as the advocacy and promotion respects the rights of a people to self-determination, and as long as the available information on likely or possible long-run consequences are made known, organizations do have that right. In addition, if the organizations have reason to believe that what they promote can have important long-range consequences, they would appear to have an obligation to undertake such research as is possible for them, to determine what these consequences might be.

FREEDOM AND RISK-TAKING

The approach taken in this paper to the ethics of population limitation has been cautionary. It has accepted the primacy of freedom of choice as a given and has suggested that the burden of proof must lie with proposals, policies or programs which would place the primacy elsewhere. At the same time, it has laid down numerous conditions necessary to discharge the burden of proof. Indeed, they are so numerous, and the process of ethical justification so difficult, that the possibility of undertaking decisive action may seem to have been excluded. This is a reasonable concern, particularly if it is the case that time is short. Is it reasonable to give the ethical advantage to freedom of choice?[44] Does this not mean that a great chance is being taken? Is it not unethical to take risks of that sort, and all the more so since others rather than ourselves will have to bear the burden if the risk-taking turns out disastrously? In particular, would it not be irresponsible for governments to take risks of this magnitude?

Three kinds of response are possible in answer to these questions. First, as mentioned, it can and has been argued that freedom of choice has hardly been given an adequate test. The absence of a safe, effective and cheap contraceptive has been one hindrance, particularly in developing countries; it is reasonable to expect that such a contraceptive will eventually be developed. The weakness of existing family planning programs (and population policies dependent upon them) has in great part been the result of inadequate financing, poor administration and scanty research and survey data. These are correctible deficiencies, assuming that nations give population limitation a high priority. If they do not give it a high priority, it will in any case be unlikely that more drastic population policies could successfully be introduced or implemented. Very little effort has been expended anywhere in the world to educate and persuade people to change their procreation habits. Until a full-scale effort has been made, there are few good grounds for asserting that it will be ineffective.

Second, while the question of scientific/medical/techno-
logical readiness, political viability, administrative feasibility,
economic capability and assumed effectiveness of proposals
which would go "beyond family planning" is not directly
ethical in nature, it has some important ethical implications.
If it seems the case that all of these categories militate against
the practical possibility of instituting very strong, immediate
or effective coercive measures, then it could become irresponsible to press for or support them. This would especially
be the case if it diverted attention away from what could be
done, e.g., an intensification of family planning programs.

Third, primacy has been given to freedom of choice for
ethical reasons. Whether this freedom will work as a means
of population limitation is a separate question. A strong indi-
cation that it will be ineffective does not, by itself, establish
grounds for rejecting it. Only if it can be shown that its failure
to reduce population growth threatens other important
human values, thus establishing a genuine conflict of values,
would the way be open to remove it from a place of primacy.
This is only another way of asserting that freedom of choice
is a right, grounded in a commitment to human dignity. The
concept of a "right" becomes meaningless if rights are wholly
subject to tests of economic, social or demographic utility, to
be given or withheld depending upon their effectiveness in
serving social goals.

In this sense, to predicate human rights at all is to take a
risk. It is to assert that the respect to be accorded human
beings ought not to be dependent upon majority opinion, cost-
benefit analysis, social utility, governmental magnanimity or
popular opinion. While it is obviously necessary to adjudicate
conflicts among rights, and often to limit one right in order
to do justice to another, the pertinent calculus is that of rights,
not of utility. A claim can be entered against the primacy of
one right only in the name of one or more other important
rights. The proper route to a limitation of rights is not directly
from social (demographic, economic, etc.) facts to rights, as if

these facts are enough in themselves to prove the case against a right. The proper route is by showing first that the social facts threaten rights, and in what way, and then showing that a limitation of one right may be necessary to safeguard or enhance other rights. To give primacy to the right of free choice is to take a risk. The justification for the risk is the high value assigned to the right, a value which transcends straight utilitarian considerations.

NOTES

1. Erik H. Erikson, *Insight and Responsibility*, W. W. Norton, New York, 1964, p. 132.

2. Bernard Berelson, "Is There an Optimum Level of Population?" in S. Fred Singer, ed., *Is There an Optimum Level of Population?*, The Population Council, forthcoming, 1971.

3. See, for instance, Paul R. Ehrlich and Anne H. Ehrlich, *Population, Resources, Environment*, W. H. Freeman and Co., San Francisco, 1970, pp. 321-324.

4. A 1967 survey undertaken by the Gallup Organization, for example, revealed that while 54% of those surveyed felt that the rate of American population growth posed a serious problem, crime, racial discrimination and poverty were thought to be comparatively more serious social problems. "American Attitudes on Population Policy: Recent Trends," in *Studies in Family Planning*, No. 30, May 1968, p. 6.

5. P. H. Nowell-Smith, *Ethics*, New York, Penguin Books, 1954, p. 11.

6. *Ibid.*, p. 12.

7. Ralph B. Potter, Jr., in the manuscript of a book edited by Leon Kass and Daniel Callahan, *Freedom, Coercion and the Life Sciences*, 1971, forthcoming.

8. Kenneth E. Boulding, "Economics as a Moral Science," *The American Economic Review*, 59, March 1969, p. 1.

9. This is the thrust of Garrett Hardin in "The Tragedy of the Commons," *Science*, 162, December 13, 1968, especially when he says (pp. 1246–1247) that "It is a mistake to think that we can control the breeding of mankind in the long run by an appeal to conscience. . . . The larger question we should ask is whether, as a matter of policy, we should ever encourage the use of a technique the tendency (if not the intention) of which is psychologically pathogenic." It is thus a short step to his recommendation of "mutual coercion, mutually agreed upon

by the majority of the people affected." (*Ibid.*, p. 1247.) See also Kingsley Davis, "Population Policy: Will Current Programs Succeed?" *Science*, 158, November 10, 1967, especially his comment that "Logically, it does not make sense to use *family* planning to provide *national* population control or planning. The 'planning' in family planning is that of each separate couple." (p. 732.)

10. See, for instance, the frequency of this theme in the Black Muslim newspaper, *Muhammad Speaks, passim.*

11. William K. Frankena, *Ethics*, Prentice-Hall, Engelwood Cliffs, N. J., 1963, p. 11.

12. *Ibid.*, p. 13.

13. *Ibid.*, p. 14.

14. *Ibid.*, p. 29.

15. *Ibid.*, p. 31.

16. *Ibid.*, p. 35.

17. Henry David Aiken, *Reason and Conduct*, Alfred A. Knopf, New York, 1962, p. 310. Aiken's argument that liberty can not and should not be defended on utilitarian grounds is worth citing in the context of this paper: "The moral foundation of liberty, I contend, is nothing other than the right to be at liberty itself. In short, the fountainhead of freedom (if the phrase may be allowed) is not utility but simply and solely the principle that every person has a right to be at liberty. . . . What authenticates it is merely our own conscientious avowal of it. In the language of Kant, the principle of liberty is categorically imperative." (*Ibid.*, p. 311.)

18. *Final Act of the International Conference on Human Rights*, United Nations, 1968, p. 15. See also the "Declaration on Population: The World Leaders Statement," in *Studies in Family Planning*, No. 26, January 1968, pp. 1–3.

19. For instance, not only has Garrett Hardin, in response to the "The World Leaders Statement" (*Ibid.*), denied the right of the family to choice with regard to family size, he has also said that "If we love the truth we must openly deny the validity of the Universal Declaration of Human Rights, even though it is promoted by the United Nations." (Hardin, *Ibid.*, p. 1246.) How literally is one to take this statement? The Declaration, after all, affirms such rights as life, liberty, dignity, equality, education, privacy and freedom of thought. Are none of these rights valid?

20. *Final Act of the International Conference on Human Rights, Ibid.*

21. *Cf.* A. S. Parkes, "The Right to Reproduce in an Overcrowded World," in F. J. Ebling, ed., *Biology and Ethics*, Academic Press, New York, 1969, pp. 109–116.

22. See Bernard Berelson, "Beyond Family Planning," *Studies in Family Planning*, No. 38, February 1969.

23. For a fuller discussion of the ethical problems of legalized abortion see, for instance, Robert E. Hall, ed., *Abortion in a Changing World*, Columbia University Press, New York, 1970, vol. 1, *passim*; and Daniel Callahan, *Abortion: Law, Choice and Morality*, The Macmillan Company, New York, especially Chapter 14. The present status of abortion laws throughout the world is detailed in Emily C. Moore, "Abortion: What is Known?" The Population Council, forthcoming, 1971.

24. Berelson, "Beyond Family Planning," *op. cit.*, p. 2.

25. Ehrlich and Ehrlich, *op. cit.*, p. 256.

26. *Ibid.*, p. 274.

27. "Universal Declaration of Human Rights," article 5, in *Human Rights: A Compilation of International Instruments of the United Nations*, United Nations, 1967.

28. Berelson, "Beyond Family Planning," *op. cit.*, p. 2.

29. *Cf.* Edward Pohlman and Kamala Gopal Rao, "Some Ethical Questions about Family Planning and Cash Incentives," *The Licentiate*, 17, 1967, pp. 236–241.

30. See, for instance, Ronald G. Ridker, "Synopsis of a Proposal for a Family Planning Bond," in *Studies in Family Planning*, No. 43, June 1969, pp. 11–16.

31. The payments made in six different family planning programs are listed in *Incentive Payments in Family Planning Programmes*, International Planned Parenthood Federation, London, 1969, pp. 8–9.

32. Berelson, "Beyond Family Planning," *op. cit.*, p. 2.

33. Garrett Hardin, "Multiple Paths to Population Control," *Family Planning Perspectives*, 2, June 1970, p. 26.

34. Berelson, "Beyond Family Planning," *op. cit.*, pp. 2–3.

35. See, for example, Wayne H. Davis, "More or Less People," *The New Republic*, June 20, 1970, pp. 19–21; and Paul R. Ehrlich, *The Population Bomb*, Ballantine Books, New York, 1968, pp. 158–173.

36. See the "International Covenant on Economic, Social and Cultural Rights," I:1,1, in *Human Rights: A Compilation of International Instruments of the United Nations, op. cit.*, p. 4: "All people have the right to self-determination. By virtue of that right they freely determine their political status and freely pursue their economic, social and cultural development."

37. "Universal Declaration of Human Rights," *op. cit.*, Article 3: "Everyone has the right to life, liberty and the security of person."

38. One of the few recent discussions on the obligation owed to future generations is in Martin P. Golding, "Ethical Issues in Biological Engineering," *UCLA Law Review*, 15, February 1968, pp. 457–463.

CAMROSE LUTHERAN COLLEGE Library

HQ
766
C25 / 21,620

39. "Universal Declaration of Human Rights," *op. cit.*

40. See Dorothy Nortman, "Population and Family Planning Programs: A Factbook," in *Reports on Population/Family Planning*, December 1969. Judith Blake expresses a pessimistic viewpoint on the possibilities of family planning programs in "Demographic Science and the Redirection of Population Policy," *Journal of Chronic Diseases*, 18, 1965, pp. 1181–1200. *Cf.* Judith Blake, "Population Policy for Americans: Is the Government Being Misled?" *Science*, 164, May 2, 1969, pp. 522–529; and the reply of Oscar Harkavy, Frederick S. Jaffe, Samuel M. Wishik, "Family Planning and Public Policy: Who Is Misleading Whom?" *Science*, 165, July 25, 1969, pp. 367–373.

41. *Cf.* Edward Pohlman, "Mobilizing Pressures Toward Small Families," *Eugenics Quarterly*, 13, June 1966, p. 122: "The spectre of 'experts' monkeying around with such private matters as family size desires frightens many people as being too 'Big Brotherish.' But those involved in eugenics, or psychotherapy, or child psychology, or almost any aspect of family planning are constantly open to the charge of interfering in private lives, so that the charge would not be new. . . . Of course, many injustices have been done with the rationale of being 'for their own good.' But the population avalanche may be used to justify—perhaps rationalize—contemplation of large-scale attempts to manipulate family size desires, even rather stealthily." This mode of reasoning may explain how some people will think and act; but it does not constitute anything approaching an ethical justification.

42. Some critical issues in the development and testing of contraceptives are discussed in Carl Djerassi, "Prognosis for the Development of New Chemical Birth-Control Agents," *Science*, 166, October 24, 1969, pp. 468–473. Djerassi argues that present FDA standards are too stringent with regard to the testing of chemical contraceptives. Two useful articles on the general problem of drug testing are Bernard Barber, "Experimenting with Humans," *The Public Interest*, Winter 1967, pp. 91–102, and Joseph F. Sadusk, Jr., "Drugs and the Public Safety," *Annals of Internal Medicine*, 65, October 1966, pp. 849–856.

43. I am indebted to J. Mayone Stycos for this suggestion, made in a seminar on ethics and population limitation at The Population Council, January 12, 1970.

44. In *The Population Bomb, op. cit.*, pp. 197–198, Paul R. Ehrlich argues that the taking of strong steps now to curb population growth is the wiser and safer gamble than doing nothing or too little. This seems to me a reasonable enough position, up to a point. That point would come when the proposed steps would be such as to seriously endanger human dignity; an ethic of survival, at the cost of other basic human values, is not worth the cost.